One Step, No Prep

Quick and Easy **SPONGE** Activities to Make the Most of Every Minute

Written by

Jo Fitzpatrick

Editor

Joel Kupperstein

Illustrator

Darcy Tom

Designer

Moonhee Pak

Project Director

Carolea Williams

Table of Contents

Introduction

Every teacher has some of those "Now what do I do?" moments when an activity ends much sooner than expected, an assembly is canceled at the last minute, or there is just not enough time to prepare for a specific activity. *One Step, No Prep* is designed for just these kinds of situations. It provides 98 math and language arts activities that can be instantly implemented. They require no last-minute preparation or setup, and the procedures are clear and simple. Best of all, these activities help you make the most out of every instructional minute in the school day.

Organization

The games in this resource are adaptable to fit neatly into your daily schedule and meet the specific needs of review and transition times. The activities are organized into three categories:

Warm-up Games are for times when students enter the classroom, after a break, or at the start of a new activity. Use the moments before students enter the room to gather necessary materials.

In-between Games are appropriate for "leftover" time, as a filler between activities or subjects, or at any other gap in the day's schedule.

Transition Games are activities in which students' participation or response grants them permission to line up, leave the classroom, or move to the next activity or setting. To speed up these games, you may wish to have students line up in pairs.

As you look at the games, you will see that many are adaptable to any of the three categories. Students' needs and the amount of time available will help determine your best use of each game.

Materials

The majority of activities in this book either require no materials at all or only materials commonly found in a classroom: paper, pencils, chalk, chalkboard, overhead projector, overhead pens, and the like. (These items are not included in activities' materials lists.) Some games do use manipulatives and charts commonly found in classrooms or materials that can be conveniently stored or displayed continuously, such as a direct-beam flashlight, a hanging number line, and a grab bag. These materials are featured in several different activities, so having them accessible will facilitate instant implementation of many delightful games. The following paragraphs describe the purpose, preparation, and presentation of these recurring materials.

Flash Cards

Several activities in this resource call for flash cards. These cards can contain math facts, spelling words, vocabulary words, or high-frequency words. Prepare these materials by writing the words or math facts on index cards. Use colored index cards to help categorize your information (e.g., use a different color card for each arithmetic operation), and laminate the cards you will use over and over. Use large cards for activities that require students to see them from a distance; use smaller cards for independent games, small-group games, partner games, and "grab bag" activities.

Grab Bag

A grab bag is any opaque bag large enough to hold cards or scraps of paper. Cards for grab bag games require data ranging from spelling words to numbers to portions of reproducibles. Prepare a separate grab bag for each game, label the bags according to the game or games with which they are used, and store them in an easily accessible place. Paper bags will work, but cloth or plastic bags are more durable.

Hanging Number Line

Displaying a hanging number line not only provides you with constant access to a material used in several of this book's games, it provides a reference tool for students learning numbers and math facts. Prepare the number line by hanging a length of twine across a corner of your classroom. Use clothespins to attach large number cards to the "clothesline" in sequential order. This book provides number cards (pages 62–64) you can reproduce (and enlarge, if possible) to create your hanging number line.

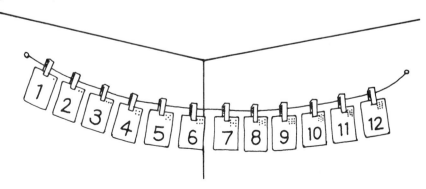

Spinners

Page 55 contains four reproducible spinners—a 0–9 spinner, a 1–10 spinner, a more/less spinner, and a blank spinner—called for by several games in this book. Photocopy these spinners onto card stock, and give a set to each student. Photocopy the spinners onto acetate, and keep a set in a folder near your overhead projector. Use the transparency spinners for whole-group activities, and invite students to use their card stock spinners when working independently. Show students how to place the point of a pencil inside a rounded end of a paper clip on the center of the spinner and spin the paper clip around the pencil point while holding the pencil in place.

Planning Ahead

After previewing the games in *One Step, No Prep*, you will see how easily these activities will fit into your curriculum with minimal effort and maximum benefit. Take the time at the beginning of the school year to collect and store close at hand the materials needed for the games. Making these materials easily accessible will improve your ability to spontaneously begin sponge activities that incorporate them. Here are some other tips for preparing your class to play these games on the spur of the moment:

🕐 Provide each student with a resealable plastic bag containing 20 linking cubes, ten of one color and ten of another.

🕐 Photocopy and enlarge the Telephone Spelling reproducible (page 61). Laminate it and have it ready for repeated use. Store it with wipe-off crayons and a cloth rag for erasing.

🕐 Create reusable overhead transparencies for games you play frequently by photocopying reproducibles found in this book onto acetate or by using permanent markers to draw game materials on acetate. Label and store these transparencies in folders near your projector for quick and easy access. Use erasable overhead pens to play these games.

To effectively implement these games, familiarize yourself and your students with the procedures. At the beginning of the year, select a handful of games to introduce and practice with students. Be sure to set your standards and expectations for conduct during the games as you introduce them. Post a list of the games so students can help select the ones they play during those "Now what do I do?" moments. Once students are familiar with the games, you will have no trouble adapting them to fit students' growing knowledge and skills.

Block Letter Crosswords

One Step, No Prep © 1999 Creative Teaching Press

Materials ⏱ none

Draw a block letter on the chalkboard. (Straight-edged letters such as *E, F, L,* and *T* work best.) Divide the letter into boxes to create a crossword puzzle. Have students brainstorm words that fit into the puzzle. Complete the puzzle as a class.

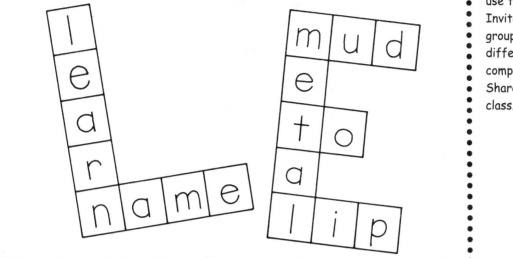

Teacher Tip

Conduct the activity in cooperative learning groups. Have each group draw and complete a puzzle made from a letter you designate. (Ask all groups to use the same letter.) Invite more advanced groups to see how many different ways they can complete the puzzle. Share the solutions as a class.

Browse and Find

One Step, No Prep © 1999 Creative Teaching Press

Materials ⏱ reading book

As students get ready to read a new story, use this activity to help them focus on the new words in the story. Have students turn to a designated page in the story and browse the page. Then, ask them to find specific words. Give clues to help students find the words (e.g., phonetic or structural clues, synonyms, or antonyms). For example:

⏱ Find a word that means *large*.

⏱ Find a word that has the little word *and* in it.

⏱ Find the word that has the *oi* sound in it.

⏱ Find the word that means the opposite of *hard-working*.

Teacher Tip

Invite students to browse and find words in the story for which they would like to make up clues. Have them write the clues during their free time or as homework. Use these clues the next time students read the story.

First and Last

Materials ⏱ blank spinner (page 55)

Create a spinner with two sections labeled *beginning* and *end*. Divide the class into three or four teams. Write the digraphs *th, ch,* and *sh* on the chalkboard. Have the first team choose a digraph. Then, spin the spinner. If the spinner comes up *beginning,* the team must think of a word with the digraph at the beginning. If the spinner comes up *end,* the team must think of a word with the digraph at the end. Give the team a point for a correct answer.

> **Teacher Tip**
>
> For less advanced students, provide a word list. This gives these students reinforcement in identifying sounds and reading words. This game is easily adaptable for individual letters or sounds other than digraphs.

Full House

Materials ⏱ Word Families reproducibles (pages 56–59)

In advance, select word family rimes you wish to use. (A word's rime is the first vowel and all the letters that follow. For example, *ick* is the rime in *trick.*) Refer to the Word Families reproducibles for ideas. Draw a house on the chalkboard for each rime. Make the house portion large enough to write in, and label the roof with the rime. Divide the class into teams of three or four players, and assign each team a house. Conduct a relay race in which players from each team take turns writing a word in their house. Declare the team whose players each write a word in their house first the winner. After the game is finished, have the class check each house for accurate spelling and read the words aloud.

> **Teacher Tip**
>
> For more advanced students, count the letters in each word rather than just the words to determine the winner. This will encourage students to use blends, clusters, and word endings.

Initial Vowel Relay

Materials ⏱ none

Divide the class into relay teams. Divide the chalkboard into columns, one for each relay team, and write the letter *a* at the top of each one. Line up a team in front of each column. Explain to students that they are to think of a word that begins with the short *a* sound and, when it is their turn, write it in their column. However, if a word already appears on their team's list, it cannot be used again. They must think of a word that has not been used. The first team to have each player write a correctly spelled word wins. Have the class read each team's list of words.

Team 1	Team 2	Team 3
a	a	a
at	apple	alligator
ax	and	after
		answer

Teacher Tip

If students tend to copy other teams' lists, give each team a different vowel sound. If you give each team the same vowel, repeat the game using a new vowel sound. This game is easily adaptable for many other skills, including long vowels, blends, and synonyms.

Letter Links

Materials ⏱ none

Assign each student a letter of the alphabet. Depending on the number of students in your class, omit difficult consonants (i.e., *q, x, z*) and vowels. Choose a theme or setting (e.g., zoo, store, circus, beach), and challenge students to name a related item that begins with their letter.

Teacher Tip

Ask students to think of an adjective (or two) that can describe their word. Challenge them to think of adjectives that also begin with their designated letter to create alliterative phrases (e.g., *big blue balloons*).

Puzzle Me a Word

Materials ⏱ Puzzle Grid reproducible (page 60), grab bag

Prior to the lesson, photocopy the reproducible grid (on card stock, if possible). Write words very lightly in the boxes, one letter per box. Write "tall" letters (i.e., *b, d, f, h, k, l, t*) and letters with a "tail" (i.e., *g, j, p, q, y*) in two vertical boxes. Cut out these word "puzzles" prior to the activity. Put the puzzles in a grab bag and list all the grab bag words on the chalkboard. Select a student to choose a puzzle from the grab bag and show it to the class. Invite students to guess the word, and have the person who guesses correctly lead the class in spelling it. Ask this student to choose another puzzle from the grab bag.

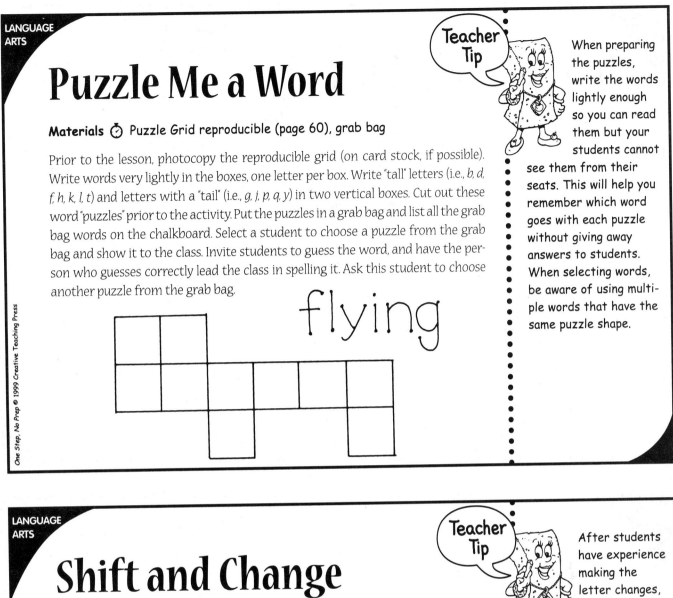

Teacher Tip

When preparing the puzzles, write the words lightly enough so you can read them but your students cannot see them from their seats. This will help you remember which word goes with each puzzle without giving away answers to students. When selecting words, be aware of using multiple words that have the same puzzle shape.

Shift and Change

Materials ⏱ none

Have students add, omit, or substitute letters in a given word to make new words. Orally give a brief prompt (e.g., *Drop the c from* crow or *Add a* b *to* oat). Do not include in your prompt the phrases *the word* or *to the word* because these extra words may divert students' attention away from the auditory blending process.

Teacher Tip

After students have experience making the letter changes, increase the difficulty by giving definitions instead of words. For example, you might say *Change the b in* boat *to make a word that is something you wear in cold weather.* This requires students to combine phonetic and semantic clues to come up with an appropriate response.

Spelling Stairs

Materials ⏱ none

Draw a box on the chalkboard. Have a student choose a letter, and write it in the box. Draw two same-sized boxes horizontally under the first one. Write the same letter in the first box. Ask students to suggest a second letter for the second box that could, in combination with the first letter, begin a word. Write that letter in the second box. Draw three boxes under the existing boxes, forming a staircase pattern, and write in the first two letters. Ask a volunteer to name a letter for the third box. Continue in this fashion until a word is made. Initially, this should be done as a teacher-guided activity in which you walk the students through the thinking process aloud. Depending on your students' ability level, use consonant-vowel-consonant words, spelling words, or high-frequency words.

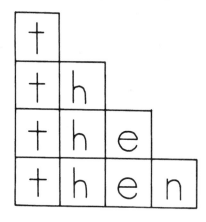

Teacher Tip

Conduct this activity with students in pairs. Give everyone the same first letter. After the activity is completed, have the pairs share the word they built. See which pair came up with the longest word. Extend the activity by challenging more advanced students to add letters before as well as after the given letter. This encourages use of polysyllabic words, prefixes, and suffixes.

One Step, No Prep © 1999 Creative Teaching Press

Stretch It

Materials ⏱ none

Introduce this activity by stating a simple sentence containing only a "who" and a "what" (e.g., *The puppy barks*). Explain to students that they are going to "stretch" the sentence by adding more details. Write the question words *When, Where,* and *Why* on the chalkboard. Ask students to suggest words that could be added to the sentence to make it longer. As students share their ideas, point to the question word that labels what they are saying.

Teacher Tip

Do this activity orally to give students practice expanding sentences. With repeated practice, students will be better able to compose complex sentences in their daily writing. If you have additional time at the end of the game or at other points in the day, invite students to illustrate their "stretched-out" sentence.

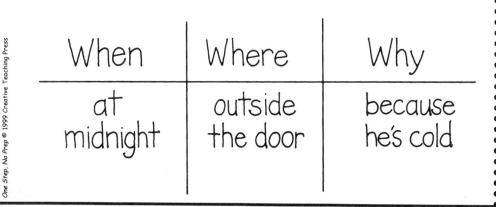

When	Where	Why
at midnight	outside the door	because he's cold

One Step, No Prep © 1999 Creative Teaching Press

Super Sleuth

Materials ⏱ none

Write a long word on the chalkboard, and ask students to use the letters in the word in any order to form new words. List all the new words on the board. After a designated amount of time, have students stop and determine their score. Give one-letter words one point, two-letter words two points, and so on. When students are ready to work without your assistance, have them play the game in cooperative groups.

an	plan	hen	lean	tape
ant	peel	pen	leap	tale
pan	he	ten	heel	plate
tan	heat	teen	teal	plant

Teacher Tip

When working with emerging readers and writers, select words that have shorter words within them (e.g., *visitor* or *upsetting*), compound words, and words with multiple vowel sounds. Students may need plenty of modeling and guided practice. Invite them to use calculators or counting boards to tally their scores if they wish.

Telephone Spelling

Materials ⏱ word list, Telephone Spelling reproducible (page 61)

Display a list of theme-related words, weekly spelling words, or high-frequency words. Have students read and copy the words. Display the telephone chart, and challenge students to predict which word might have the highest point value based on the numbers that coordinate with its letters. Then, have students determine each word's point value, and write it next to the word.

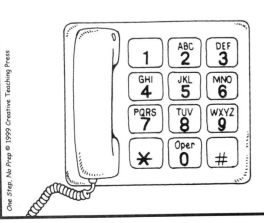

bold

$2+6+5+3=16$

Teacher Tip

Start out slowly so the students benefit from the spelling practice and the addition of points. Invite students to use manipulatives, counting boards, or calculators to help them count points.

Word Boxing

Materials ⏱ none

Draw a six-by-six grid on an overhead projector transparency. Divide the class into two teams, and give each team a different-colored overhead marker. Select a volunteer from each team to begin the game. Have each player write a letter in a box and pass the marker to a teammate. Ask these and the following players to take turns adding letters to the boxes with the goal of completing a word vertically or horizontally. Have the player who writes the last letter of a word claim it by coloring over the word with his or her team's designated color. This game requires high-level thinking strategies, as players must watch the screen to complete words and try to block the other team at the same time.

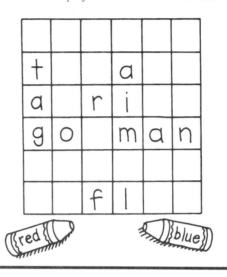

One Step, No Prep © 1999 Creative Teaching Press

Teacher Tip

Invite students to refer to a word bank or a weekly spelling-word list to select words. **As students' skills progress, have them use larger grids.** Once they are familiar with the rules and strategies of the game, invite students to play against partners instead of in large teams.

Word Extensions

Materials ⏱ none

Write a theme-related word vertically on the chalkboard with each letter in a box. Ask students to think of and dictate to you a sentence related to the theme that contains a word beginning with a letter in one of the boxes. Have students read each sentence after you write it. After all the sentences have been written, read them together as a story.

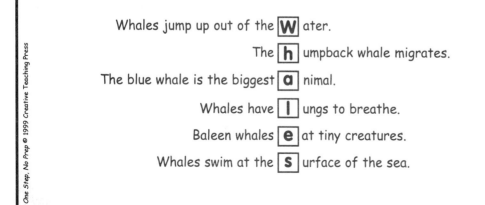

Whales jump up out of the W ater.

The h umpback whale migrates.

The blue whale is the biggest a nimal.

Whales have l ungs to breathe.

Baleen whales e at tiny creatures.

Whales swim at the s urface of the sea.

Teacher Tip

Use colored chalk to write the theme-related word. Encourage students to think about the topic and brainstorm other theme-related words that begin with each letter. This is a great way to provide review using high-level thinking skills. It is also a great way to familiarize the class with students' names at the beginning of the school year.

One Step, No Prep © 1999 Creative Teaching Press

Word Family Whirl

One Step, No Prep © 1999 Creative Teaching Press

Materials ⏲ Word Families reproducibles (pages 56–59)

Draw on the chalkboard a spiral large enough to write words on the line. Choose a word that contains a word family rime. (See the Word Families reproducibles for ideas.) Write the word on the outer edge of the spiral and the rime in the center. Ask students to think of words to add to the "word family whirl." Have students spell each word as you write it on the whirl.

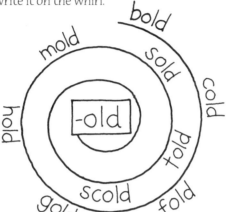

Teacher Tip

Draw and photocopy a whirl for each student, and have students race to see how many word family words they can add to their whirl. Invite volunteers to share their words. Guide students to discover that blends and letter clusters can be used to make more words.

Word Stretcher

Materials ⏲ Word Families reproducibles (pages 56–59)

One Step, No Prep © 1999 Creative Teaching Press

Write a rime from the Word Families reproducibles on the chalkboard. Demonstrate how letters can be substituted or added to the rime to form new words (e.g., adding the letter *k* to *-it* to make *kit*). Invite students to brainstorm a list of words that fit the pattern, and record their responses. Remind students that their answers must be real words, not just random letter combinations. Draw lines to connect each new word to the original rime. Make branches from the lines when the new word can be altered to form several additional words (e.g., *sit* to *skit*, *slit*, and *spit*).

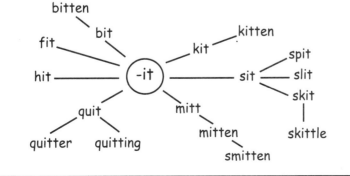

Teacher Tip

As students become comfortable with the activity, put them in pairs and have them make their own "word stretcher." See which team can come up with the most new words. When pairing students, consider putting a struggling student with a more capable one.

Addition Parade

Materials ⏱ none

Divide the class into two groups, and have the two groups line up facing each other. Leave a large space between the two lines. Say a number, and have that many students from the front of the first line step forward and join hands. Then, say another number, and have that many students from the front of the second line step forward and join hands. Say the two numbers in an addition problem, and have the group from each line walk to the middle of the room. Invite the two groups to join hands and parade between the two lines as they say the addition problem and its solution. When they finish, have them go to the end of their line.

Teacher Tip

Keep a lively pace by having students move up their lines as their class-mates walk to the center. As the designated students parade down the middle of the lines, have all the students join them in chanting the problem. This keeps everyone involved while waiting for their turn to join the parade.

Addition Relay Race

Materials ⏱ none

Divide the class into teams, and have each team line up in front of the chalkboard. Have the first person from each team write on the board a number you dictate and go to the back of his or her team's line. Dictate another number, and have the second person from each team go to the board, mentally add that number to the existing number, erase the first number, and write the answer. The first player to do this earns a point for his or her team. These students then go to the back of their team's line and the next players proceed in the same manner. End the game when all players have answered a problem.

Teacher Tip

Consider creating more teams with fewer members so more students can participate simultaneously. Because students know that their turn is coming soon, they will pay closer attention. If necessary, establish a cutoff number. When this number is reached, begin a new game. This keeps the sums within a predetermined range.

Breakaway

Materials ⏱ linking cubes, 1–10 spinner (page 55)

Give each student ten linking cubes of the same color. Spin the 1–10 spinner, and have students make a "train" of that many linking cubes. On the command *Breakaway*, have students break their train into two segments. Ask students to compare their train parts to see how many different ways they can make the number.

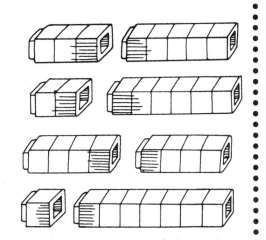

Teacher Tip

Write on the chalkboard the number the spinner lands on. As students share ways they broke their train apart, write those numbers in the form of addition problems. When all possibilities have been listed, have students read aloud the problems. As students' ability progresses, challenge them to break their train into three segments.

Clothesline Math

Materials ⏱ hanging number line

Ask students to predict which number they think will be the last number on the number line. Say an addition or subtraction problem. Have students say the answer simultaneously, and remove the answer's number card. Continue playing until only one card remains.

Teacher Tip

Continue using problems whose answers have been removed from the number line. Students will get extra review and they may more readily remember the answer because it can no longer be used in the game. If students need visual reinforcement, use flash cards instead of saying the problem orally. After completing the game, play again in reverse, hanging the answers back on the number line.

Fair Share

Materials ⏱ linking cubes, construction paper

Provide each student with 20 linking cubes. Have each student draw a given number of large stick figures on a piece of construction paper. Tell students a number 20 or less, and ask them to divide that many linking cubes so that each stick figure gets a fair share (the same amount). Ask students how they can be sure that each person gets the same amount.

Teacher Tip

Encourage students as they work to discover other ways of grouping and distributing the designated number of linking cubes. This will help you lead students to discover different multiplication facts that have the same solution, such as 3 × 4 and 2 × 6.

Looking for Patterns

Materials ⏱ none

To help students practice number patterning skills, recite story problems such as the following:

⏱ *Phillip loves to catch tadpoles in the nearby pond. The first time he put his net in the pond he caught two tadpoles. The second time he put his net into the water, four tadpoles swam into it. The third time, he caught six tadpoles in his net. How many tadpoles did he catch the fourth time he put his net into the water?*

⏱ *Ms. Jones loves to read stories to her class. On Monday, she read one story. On Tuesday, she read three stories. On Wednesday, she read five stories, and on Thursday, she read seven stories. How many stories will she read on Friday?*

Teacher Tip

To help students understand how these number patterns work, show them a pattern in which one of the numbers has been left out (e.g., 2, 4, ___, 8). Ask students what the missing number is and how they know this. To increase the challenge of the activity, give students the number pattern, and ask them to make up a story problem that corresponds to it.

Patterning

Materials ⏱ pattern blocks

Divide the class into groups, and have each group stand around a table. (If your students sit in cooperative groups, have them stand around their desk clusters.) Place an assortment of pattern blocks in the middle of each table, and ask students to make a pattern using three blocks. On your signal, have students move to their neighbor's place and continue that person's pattern. Have students continue rotating and adding to patterns until they are back at their original starting points.

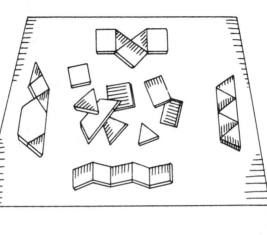

Teacher Tip

Establish the direction and have students practice rotating before they actually begin patterning. This will allow for a smoother flow during the activity. As the students' patterning skills progress, increase the number of blocks to be used or give a designated pattern to follow (e.g., A A B C C).

The Place Value Game

Materials ⏱ spinners (page 55)

Draw three sets of three boxes on the chalkboard. Label each set *ones, tens,* and *hundreds.* Divide the class into three teams, and line up each team in front of a set of boxes. Have the first player from each team go to the board. Spin the 0–9 spinner, and have each player place the number in the box of their choice—ones, tens, or hundreds. Spin the spinner twice more, and have a new player from each team place each of these numbers. After all the numbers are in the boxes, have the class determine which is the largest number and which is the smallest. Spin the more/less spinner. If it comes up *more,* give a point to the team with the highest number. If it comes up *less,* give a point to the team with the lowest number. If more than one team comes up with the winning number, give each team a point.

Teacher Tip

For a quieter activity, divide the class into pairs, and have students write numbers on scratch paper. Use the more/less spinner to determine the winner in each pair.

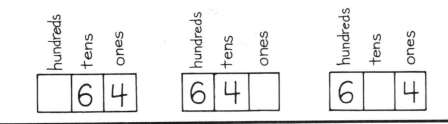

Place Value Grab Bag

Teacher Tip

Increase the difficulty of the activity by writing the place value numbers in random order. For example, you might write *8 ones, 1 hundred, 4 tens*. This requires students to remember the numbers and put them in the correct place value sequence. You may also wish to include numbers such as 203 so students gain experience with the place value of 0. To keep all students involved, have them write the answer on scratch paper.

Materials ⏱ expanded-number cards, grab bag

Prior to the lesson, write some expanded numbers on index cards or sentence strips (e.g., *1 hundred, 4 tens, 8 ones*). Place the expanded-number cards in a grab bag, and have a student choose a card. Have the student read what the card says. Invite a volunteer to write the numerical form of the number on the chalkboard and select the next card from the grab bag.

Show Me the Facts

Teacher Tip

Depending on the ability level of your students, consider using flash cards or problems written on the chalkboard to provide visual cues.

Materials ⏱ 1–12 number cards (pages 62–64)

Distribute a set of number cards to each student. Ask students to spread out the cards in order on their desk. Explain that they will be practicing math facts without using their voices. Call out a math problem, and then ask students to mentally solve the problem and hold up the card with the answer.

One Step, No Prep © 1999 Creative Teaching Press

MATH

Spin a Problem

Materials ⏱ blank spinner (page 55)

Prepare a spinner that contains numbers and operation signs (e.g., +3, -4, -6). Have a student select a number between 1 and 6. Then, spin the spinner, and have students do the appropriate computation. If the problem cannot be done, discuss why and spin again. An example of this activity might proceed as follows:

⏱ The beginning number is 4. The spinner lands on +1. Students say *five*. Spinning again, the spinner lands on -6. The students decide that the problem cannot be done because six is more than five. Spin again. The spinner lands on -3. The students answer *two*, and so on.

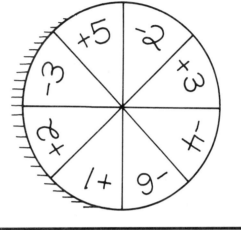

Teacher Tip

Select numbers less than 6 to emphasize the concept of subtracting a smaller number from a larger number. Use numbers 10 or greater as the initial number to review general addition and subtraction. You may wish to assign a student recorder to write the problems on the chalkboard as you generate them.

MATH

Spinner Addition

Materials ⏱ linking cubes, blank spinner (page 55)

Give each student 20 linking cubes, ten of one color and ten of another color. Create a spinner appropriate for students' ability level: 0–3 for beginning addition, 0–6 for moderate addition, and 0–10 for more advanced addition. Spin the spinner, and have students use one color to make a linking-cube "train" of that length. Spin again, and have students use the other color to make a train of that length. Have students put their trains together and verbalize the addition problem their trains represent.

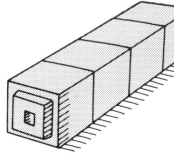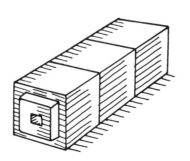

Teacher Tip

To combine the representational with the concrete, write the numbers on the chalkboard as the problem is verbalized. For more advanced students, use the missing-addend format. Explain that each train is to end up with ten "cars." Use the spinner to determine how many cars are already on the train. Ask students how many more cars are needed to make a ten-car train.

One Step, No Prep © 1999 Creative Teaching Press

Up and Down

Materials ⏱ hanging number line, pointer

Ask a student to select a number from the hanging number line. Point to that number. Ask the class to go either up or down the number line according to your direction and say the number aloud. For example, you might begin with the number 11 and say *Go down four. Now go up two. Go up two more. Now go down five.*

Teacher Tip

Begin slowly, giving students time to complete each direction. Talk through the process by labeling the operation (e.g., *We now have more* or *Now we're going to end up with less*). Introduce the terms *add* and *subtract* when appropriate. As students need less visualization, speed up or give multiple directions, such as *Go up two then down four.*

Who Wins?

Materials ⏱ spinners (page 55), linking cubes

Divide the class into two teams, and label one team the "more" team and the other the "less" team. Draw a two-column scoreboard on the chalkboard, and label it *more* and *less.* Have one team sit on the left side of the overhead projector and the other team sit on the right side. Spin a number on the 1–10 spinner, and make a linking-cube "train" of that length on the overhead projector. Spin again, and make a train of that length. Compare the two trains, and ask students which train has more and which has less. Summarize the comparison using number words (e.g., *Seven is more than four* or *Three is less than six*). Then, use the more/less spinner to determine the winner. Give a point to the winning team.

Teacher Tip

Use this game to reinforce the fact that the winner isn't always the one with the most. Use the more/less spinner with other classroom games to determine the winner. Eventually, students will become less anxious about having the most. Reiterate the point that everyone should have fun, whether they win or lose. If you wish, invite volunteers from the teams to form their linking-cube trains.

Analogy Building

Materials ⏱ none

Use analogies to help students see similarities, comparisons, and relationships between pairs of items. Begin by sharing some analogies and having the class add the last word. For example:

Dark is to night as light is to _____. *(day)*
School is to learn as recess is to _____. *(play)*
Food is to hungry as drink is to _____. *(thirsty)*
Sugar is to sweet as lemon is to _____. *(sour)*
Car is to road as airplane is to _____. *(sky)*

Invite students to make up some of their own analogies.

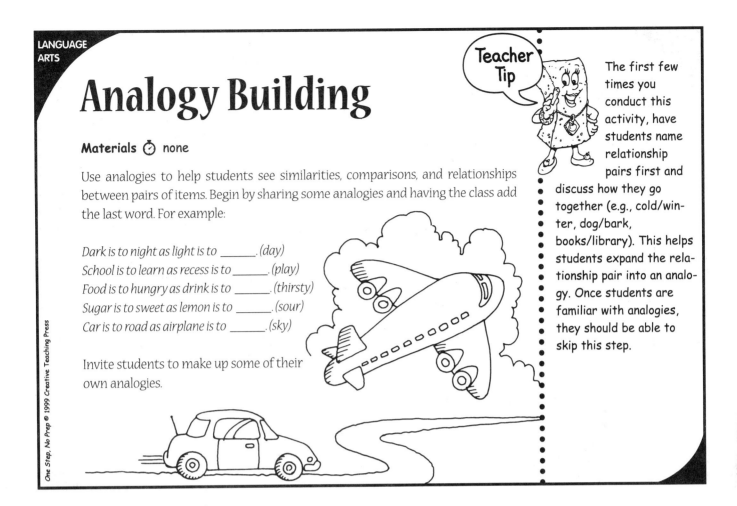

Teacher Tip

The first few times you conduct this activity, have students name relationship pairs first and discuss how they go together (e.g., cold/winter, dog/bark, books/library). This helps students expand the relationship pair into an analogy. Once students are familiar with analogies, they should be able to skip this step.

Clap and Tap Words

Materials ⏱ word list

Before beginning the activity, display a word list where students can easily see the words. Explain that students will use noises to practice spelling. Tell them that a clap indicates a consonant and a tap (on a table or desk) indicates a vowel. Demonstrate that for each clap, you will write a *c* on the chalkboard, and for each tap, you will write a *v*. Once the designated letters have been written, challenge students to use these clues to find the matching word on the list.

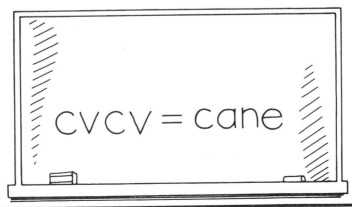

Teacher Tip

When selecting words for your list, choose words that have different letter patterns so the words can be easily identified. When students are familiar with the game, invite them to secretly choose a word from the list and provide the claps and taps as clues for their classmates.

Directed Drawing

Materials ⏱ none

When first introducing Directed Drawing, explain to students that you will give oral directions for drawing a picture and they are to follow them to see if they drew the same picture you described. For example, to have students draw a television, you might say *Draw a rectangle. Draw a square inside the rectangle, leaving space inside the rectangle on one side of the square. Draw a column of four circles inside the empty space next to the square. Draw a short straight line down from each of the bottom corners of the rectangle.* Once students understand the game, pass out drawing paper. Give each direction and model every step of the way.

Teacher Tip

Have students use fine-point markers to prevent them from missing important steps because they were pre-occupied with erasing. When students are familiar with the game, have them play in pairs with one person giving the directions and the other person drawing the picture.

Directional Spelling

Materials ⏱ graph paper

Draw a three-by-three grid on the chalkboard. Write a three-letter word across the top of the grid, one letter in each box. Add the last two letters down the left side to make the same word. Have students copy the grid on graph paper and fill in the remaining squares so there are three correctly spelled words in the horizontal boxes.

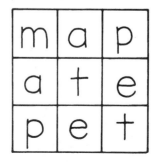

Teacher Tip

For a real challenge, repeat the activity so the horizontal and vertical boxes must contain correctly spelled words. Attempting to complete the puzzle in this manner may take more time. Consider leaving the grid on the board or placing a copy of it in a learning center so students can work on it during their free time. As students gain proficiency with this game, have them work with four-by-four grids.

Facts in Five

Materials ⏱ none

Draw a large three-by-five grid on the chalkboard. Label the left side of the grid with five letters of the alphabet and the top with three categories. Ask students to brainstorm an example of each category that starts with each letter. Write the responses in the appropriate boxes. Once students have a feel for the game, have them play individually or in small groups. Give students time to write responses independently, and then ask volunteers to share what they wrote. See which responses were commonly suggested and which appeared on only one student's list.

	Food	Animal	TV
S	salad	snake	
m	macaroni		Mister Rogers
c		cat	cartoons
p	peas	panda	
t	tomato	toad	

Teacher Tip

For less advanced students, use color words instead of letters and only two simple categories, such as "outside things" and "inside things." Conduct the game as an oral activity, but write responses on the board so students see the print connection. Also, you can invite them to draw pictures of their answers instead of writing words.

Finish Me

Materials ⏱ none

Introduce the activity by telling the students that you are going to give them a part of a word (a detached syllable) and that they are to figure out what the word could be. For example, you might say *fen* (fender), *thim* (thimble), *chat* (chatter), or *wob* (wobble). Choose difficult vocabulary words from shared and guided reading stories to help students become more familiar with them. When they meet these words in print, they will have an easier time deciphering the words.

Teacher Tip

Have students clap out the syllables of the words until they are proficient at syllable counting. For more advanced students, use syllables other than the first one. Encourage students to come up with multiple possibilities for the same detached syllable.

thim___

Grab Bag Spelling

Materials ⏱ grab bag, word cards

Have students take turns choosing a word card from the grab bag and reading it aloud. Challenge each student to write the word correctly on a piece of scratch paper. Invite the student who selected the word to write the correct spelling on the chalkboard. To conclude the activity, have students read the list of words from the board.

Teacher Tip

Keep a lively pace and high interest by making teaching comments. For example, you might say *I hear /ch/ in that word* or *Remember which long i spelling usually ends with a t.* The clues will help struggling students focus on the word, while more advanced students will already be writing it. Challenge students who finish early to write a rhyming word next to the word they just spelled.

Guess My Word

Materials ⏱ grab bag, word cards

Choose a word card from the grab bag. Write on the chalkboard a letter from the middle of the word. Ask students to guess the word. If no one guesses correctly, add another letter—either the letter before or after the letter you wrote on the board. Once again, ask students to guess the word. Continue building the word until it is guessed correctly.

Teacher Tip

If students require additional visual cues, post the word list on a wall or write it on the board.

Keep a lively pace by only allowing a few guesses after you write each letter.

I Spy

Materials ⏱ none

Have students identify "spied" objects from around the room by listening to phonemic clues. For example:

I spy an object with three sounds in its name.
I spy an object with three sounds in its name, and the first sound is /d/.
I spy an object with three sounds in its name. The first one is /d/, and the last one is /r/.
I spy an object with three sounds in its name, and it rhymes with floor.

Encourage students to guess the word after each clue.

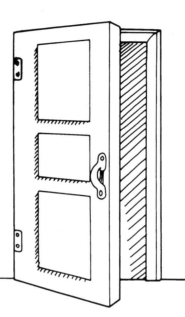

Teacher Tip

For less advanced students, add a descriptive clue with the phonemic clues. For example, *I spy an object that has three sounds in its name. The first one is /d/, and the last one is /r/. It opens and closes and rhymes with floor.* After students are familiar with the game, ask them to provide clues for their classmates.

Letter House

Materials ⏱ none

Draw a picture of a house on the chalkboard. Make it large enough to write words inside the house. On the roof section, write a short-vowel sound and random consonant sounds that could be combined to make words. Have students identify words that could be made using the vowel and beginning and ending consonants. Write the words inside the house as students say them. When finished, have students read the list of newly created words.

Teacher Tip

When determining letters to be used, think of word family words. When possible, include letters that can be used in blends to create four- or five-letter words. This activity can be played using two relay teams. When scoring, give a point for each letter in the word. This encourages students to combine letters to make longer words.

Name It

Materials ⏱ none

Select a student without telling the class who it is. Give oral clues to the identity of that student by saying words that begin with each letter of that student's name. For example, you might use *jump*, *ant*, *nut*, and *elephant* for the name *Jane*. Invite students to identify the first letter of each word and guess which student you named.

T a l l

i n c h

m a k e

Teacher Tip

As a Transition Game, have students move to their next activity after they are named. As an In-between or Warm-up Game, have named students list clues for the next student to be named. To ensure accuracy, have the student tell you the name of the new student in advance.

Oddball

Materials ⏱ none

Ask the students to listen carefully as you say three words (e.g., *ball*, *hill*, and *toy*). Explain that only two of the three words share a common sound. Challenge students to identify the word that does not belong, in this case, *toy*. Say the words one at a time, and then have students hold up one, two, or three fingers to indicate whether the first, second, or third word is the "oddball." Because multiple answers may be possible in some cases, ask students to explain why they chose the oddball that they did.

Teacher Tip

This activity can be used for many different sounds or concepts. For example, consider using words that share beginning or medial sounds, have the same number of syllables, or are synonyms. You may wish to tell students the category of the game, but omitting this information makes the game a little more challenging.

Pantomime Spelling

Materials ⏱ none

In advance, choose a category for the words you will use in this game, such as action words (verbs) or describing words (adjectives). Select a student to think of an appropriate word and act it out. Invite remaining students to guess the word. After someone guesses correctly, have the actor write the word on the chalkboard as the other students spell it. Invite the actor to choose another student to act out a new word.

fly

Teacher Tip

After you compile a list on the chalkboard, number the words. Invite a volunteer to call out a number. Ask the others to silently read and spell the word as the volunteer acts it out. More advanced students can broaden the categories and also include past spelling words.

The Pyramid Game

Materials ⏱ none

Have one student choose a letter to begin the game. Write that letter on the chalkboard. Then, ask a volunteer to add a letter to make a word. Write the two-letter word under the first letter. Continue having students add one letter at a time to make new words. See how big students can build the "pyramid."

t
to
top
stop
stoop

Teacher Tip

If you need to simplify the game, use rhyming words instead of having students create new words letter by letter. Start the pyramid by writing a word at the top. Ask students to name a word that rhymes with it. Have them spell the word as you add it to the pyramid.

Rhyming Zigzag

Materials ⏱ none

Place students in two lines facing each other. Say a word to the first person in the first line (e.g., *mat*). That student says the word to the person standing directly across from him or her. This student repeats the word and then says a "replacement" letter for the beginning sound (e.g., *mat, c*). The student standing directly across in the opposite line says the new word made by changing the first letter *(cat)*. The next student directly across then says another replacement letter, and his or her partner then makes a new word using that beginning sound. The students continue the zigzag process until every student has had a turn. If all the replacement possibilities are exhausted, give the next student a new word to use.

mat, c

cat

Teacher Tip

Establish ahead of time whether or not nonsense words are permissible. Early-fluency readers will benefit from inventing nonsense rhymes. More advanced students can be asked to make only real words. A variation of this game can be played substituting vowel or ending sounds.

One Step, No Prep © 1999 Creative Teaching Press

Sampling Similes

Materials ⏱ none

Introduce the activity by explaining that a simile is a way of comparing two very different things using the words *like* and *as*. Give an example of a simile, such as *The elephant was as big as a truck.* Ask students to complete similes such as the following:

The dog was as wet as _____.
The glue was as sticky as _____.
The cactus was as sharp as _____.
The man was as tall as _____.
The snow was as soft as _____.
The plane looked like _____.
The clouds looked like _____.

Teacher Tip

Have students make up their own similes using the format *as _____ as a _____.* Invite each student to pick a partner. Have one student choose a word for the first blank and the other student fill in the second blank.

One Step, No Prep © 1999 Creative Teaching Press

Scavenger Hunt

Materials ⏱ none

Invite students to take a mental, visual, or physical hunt around the room for items in the room that begin with each letter of the alphabet. Have them list the items in alphabetical order. The student with the most items found is the winner. This activity can also be done with students working in pairs.

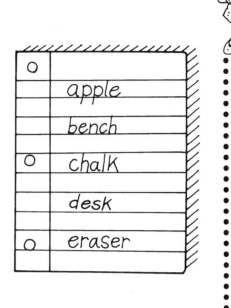

Teacher Tip

Before the activity, take an inventory of objects to see if the whole alphabet is represented. Add items in plain sight for the letters that are not already represented.

The Step Game

Materials ⏱ none

Write a three-letter word at the top of the chalkboard. Have students read the word. Ask a volunteer to say the last letter in the word and a three-letter word that starts with that letter. Write this word vertically, beginning with the last letter of the first word. Have the students read the word and identify the ending letter. Challenge another volunteer to think of a three-letter word that begins with the word's ending letter, and write it horizontally on the board. Continue in this manner, and have students watch the steps form.

```
she
  n
  dog
    e
    tap
```

Teacher Tip

This game facilitates less advanced students' accurate spelling by focusing on three-letter words. As the students become comfortable with the game, have them work in pairs or alone and time them to see how many steps they can make within a given time period. Invite more proficient spellers to use words of any length.

Stick 'Em Up

Materials ⏱ marker, small sticky notes

Write a sentence on the chalkboard that contains a subject and an object (e.g., *The cat ate the meat.*). Underline the subject and the object. Have students read the sentence, and invite them to change the sentence by substituting new letters for the initial consonant sounds of the underlined words. Write the new letters on sticky notes, and attach them on top of the old letters. After each change, have students read the new sentence.

Teacher Tip

Refer to the Word Families reproducibles (pages 56–59) to generate ideas for this activity. Have more advanced students use sentence strips and sticky notes to make their own "flip-up" sentences to share with the class.

The [r]at ate the [s]eat.

One Step, No Prep © 1999 Creative Teaching Press

Word Worm

Materials ⏱ none

Write a word on the chalkboard, and ask students to change one letter in the word to create a different word. Write the new word next to the original word. Repeat this process, writing the words in a worm-shaped arrangement. Challenge students to make the "word worm" as long as possible. Continue until they can think of no new words.

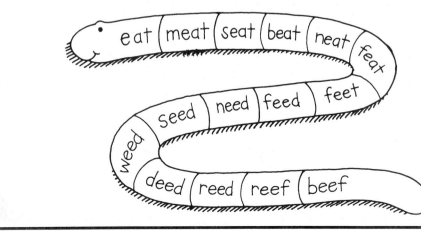

eat | meat | seat | beat | neat | feat
feet | feed | need | seed | weed
deed | reed | reef | beef

Teacher Tip

Help students discover that thinking of rhyming words may provide them with words in which the first letter has changed. If they cannot think of a rhyming word, suggest that they change the last sound. Then, they can change the beginning sound of the new word. This opens the door to another rhyming family.

One Step, No Prep © 1999 Creative Teaching Press

Backtrack

Materials ⏱ none

Draw a row of eight boxes on the chalkboard to simulate a path on a game board. Number the last four boxes with a number sequence, such as 12, 13, 14, 15. Tape a paper game-board marker on one of these numbers. Explain that you will give students "game-board moves" to make. Demonstrate by giving cues, such as *You have to move back five spaces. What number would you land on?*, and moving the marker accordingly. Give other cues, and have students mentally calculate where the marker would land. Repeat the game with a different number sequence in the last four boxes.

Teacher Tip

If students initially need the visual cue of the numbers in the empty boxes, write them in. However, over time, students should be able to do the calculations without these visual cues. This type of skill appears on many standardized tests. (Note: If tape damages your chalkboard, use magnets as markers or draw chalk marks in the boxes.)

				12	13	14	15

Calendar Addition

Materials ⏱ calendar

Pose to students math tasks that incorporate calendar-reading skills, such as the following:

⏱ Add the dates of the first Monday and the third Tuesday.

⏱ Subtract the date of the second Wednesday from the date of the last Wednesday.

⏱ How many days are between the first Monday and the fourth Thursday?

⏱ Add together all the dates in the first week.

Teacher Tip

Make sure the calendar is easily visible for all students. Consider modeling the computation on an overhead projector to aid struggling students. Invite student volunteers to suggest calendar problems for the class to solve.

Su	M	Tu	W	Th	F	Sa
		1	2	3	4	5
6	7	8	9	10	11	12
13	14	15	16	17	18	19
20	21	22	23	24	25	26
27	28	29	30	31		

$$7+15=22$$

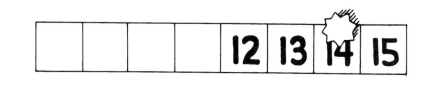

Erase It

Materials ⏱ none

Draw a three-by-four grid on the chalkboard. Number the boxes 1–12. Tell students that when an answer is given, that number will be erased from the grid. Have the students predict which number will be the last one left in the grid. Say a math problem, and have the class say the answer. Erase that number from the grid. Continue in this manner until only one number is left. See how this number corresponds to students' predictions. If their predictions were inaccurate, have students calculate how far off they were.

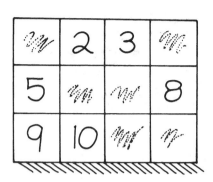

Teacher Tip

You may wish to use flash cards instead of listing problems orally to provide students with visual cues. Continue to use problems whose answers have been erased to provide additional reinforcement. Some students may even remember the problem better because the answer was already gone from the grid!

Graph It

Materials ⏱ math-fact flash cards (optional)

Draw a large grid on the chalkboard or overhead projector. Make the grid's number of columns equal to the largest solution you will work with. For example, if twelve is the largest solution of any of the math facts in your game, give the grid twelve columns. Include at least three or four rows. Number the columns across the bottom of the grid. Tell students that they are going to be in a math-facts race.

Invite them to guess which number they think will appear as a solution most often. Show a flash card or say an equation. When students say the answer, color a box above the appropriate number on the graph. Continue giving problems and filling in boxes in the graph.

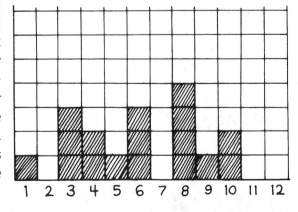

Teacher Tip

If time permits, invite a student who gave the correct answer to fill in a box on the graph. As the game continues, ask questions about the graph, such as *Which number has the most? Which has the least? How many more does ___ have than ___? How many does ___ need in order to catch up with ___? How many less does ___ have than ___?* Finally, ask students to gauge how successful their predictions were.

How Many More?

Materials ⏱ none

Write *Boys* on the left side of the chalkboard. Leave quite a bit of space, and write *Girls* in the center of the board. Leave more space, and write *Total* on the right side of the board. Have a student pick a number, and write that number under *Total*. Tell students that this number is the total number of children you must have. Choose some boys to stand under the word *Boys*. Point to the boys, and say *Now we have ____ boys, but we have to have ____ children all together. How many girls do we need?* Demonstrate the thinking process by adding one girl at a time, counting as you go until you reach the required number. Repeat the procedure until students can quickly go through the process.

Teacher Tip

Expand the procedure by writing the number sentence on the board. This demonstrates to students missing-addend arithmetic. After the class answers the problem, ask students if there are more boys or more girls, and how many more.

Boys   Girls   Total

6

One Step, No Prep © 1999 Creative Teaching Press

If Your Number ...

Materials ⏱ more/less spinner (page 55)

Ask each student to choose a number between 1 and 100 and find a partner. After students find a partner, have them tell each other their number. (Be sure no partners have the same number.) Then, spin the more/less spinner. If it lands on *more*, say *If your number is more than your partner's, sit down.* If it lands on *less*, say *If your number is less than your partner's, sit down.* Repeat the procedure with the students who are still standing. Have them find a new partner and share their numbers. Once again, spin the spinner. Continue playing until there are only two students left standing. Play one last time to see who the final winner is.

Teacher Tip

You may wish to have students write their number on a sticky note and stick it to their shirt or blouse or on scrap paper they conceal in their hand. This way, students cannot change their number in their eagerness to win.

One Step, No Prep © 1999 Creative Teaching Press

Mine!

Materials ⏱ graph-paper transparency

Explain to students that the object of this game is to win squares for yourself while blocking your opponent. To win a square, a player must trace the fourth side of the square with his or her color. When this happens, that person colors in the box.

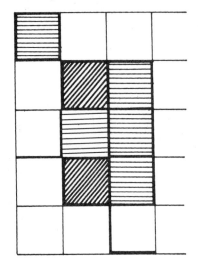

Demonstrate the game by playing with a student volunteer on an overhead projector. Give the volunteer a pen of a different color than yours. Use your pen to trace one side of a square on the grid. Have your opponent trace a side of any square he or she wishes. (Players can only trace one side of a square during a turn.) As the game continues, students will see that on any turn, a player can work toward completing a square or blocking his or her opponent. The winner is the player with the most squares colored in.

One Step, No Prep © 1999 Creative Teaching Press

Limit the size of the demonstration game to prevent it from taking too much time.

Once students are familiar with the game, invite them to pick partners and play using graph paper and crayons. You can also use larger graph paper and increase the number of players. This way, students will quickly learn strategies for outmaneuvering their opponents.

One, Two, Skiperoo

Materials ⏱ direct-beam flashlight, hanging number line

Have students practice skip counting with this activity. Shine a flashlight on a number in the number line, skip the next number, and shine it on the following number until you reach the end of the number line. Have the students say the numbers as they are spotlighted. Count up the number line several times, increasing the speed each time.

One Step, No Prep © 1999 Creative Teaching Press

Adjust the length of your number line to have students practice counting by threes, fives, and tens.

Have students just learning to skip count whisper the word *skip* in place of each number they omit (e.g., *three, skip, skip, six, skip, skip, nine, skip, skip*).

Spotlight Addition

Materials ⏱ direct-beam flashlights, hanging number line

Give two students each a flashlight. Invite one student to shine the flashlight on a number in the number line, and have the rest of the class say the number and the word *plus*. Then, ask the second student to shine the flashlight on another number. Have the class say that number to complete the addition problem. Ask the whole class to respond with the answer.

Teacher Tip

Add a third student and flashlight to create three-addend addition problems. Pause between the second and third numbers so students have time to compute the first two addends.

Spotlight Sequence

Materials ⏱ direct-beam flashlight, hanging number line

Ask the class *What number comes before (after or between). . . ?*, and shine a flashlight on a number (or numbers) in the number line. Have students respond chorally. After repeating the game for several numbers, invite student volunteers to shine the flashlight on the numbers.

Teacher Tip

When students demonstrate understanding of number sequence, alternate the directions so that the concepts of before, after, and in between are incorporated randomly. Invite students to take turns asking the questions. This activity also works well for reviewing the letters of the alphabet.

Spotlight Subtraction

Materials ⏱ direct-beam flashlights, hanging number line

Give two students each a flashlight, and ask each student to shine the flashlight on a number. As each number is spotlighted, have the rest of the class say the number. Select a third student to turn the numbers into a subtraction problem. Emphasize that when subtracting, the smaller number must be subtracted from the larger number. After the student says the subtraction problem aloud, have the rest of the class answer the problem. Continue the activity by selecting three more students to participate.

Teacher Tip

If students need help visualizing the concept, have the third student write the problem on the chalkboard. Emphasize that the bigger number must come first.

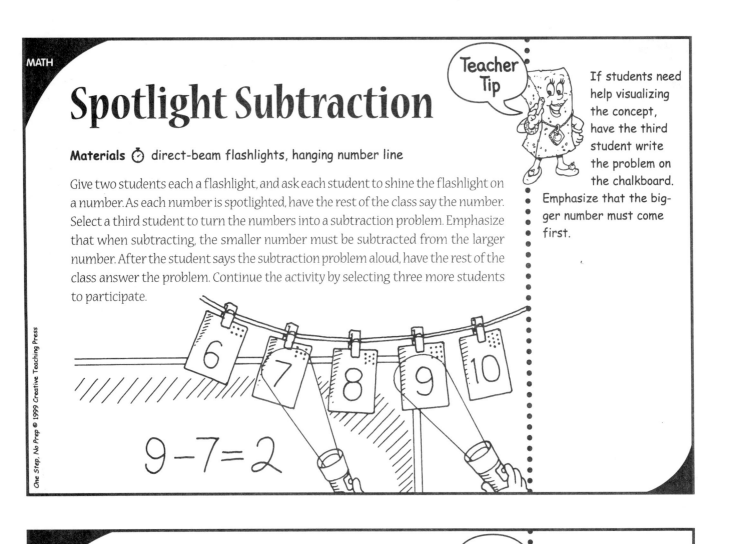

Up Two

Materials ⏱ direct-beam flashlight, hanging number line

Explain to students that each time a number is spotlighted, they are to add two to that number. Choose a student to shine a flashlight on a number, and have the rest of the class say the answer. Then, invite the student to pass the flashlight to someone who said the correct answer. (This encourages participation and gives slower students a chance to be chosen because the student selected does not have to be the first one to say the correct answer.)

Teacher Tip

This activity can be used to help students understand the concept of counting by twos. The game can also be changed to "Up Three" or "Up Four."

Use Your Cents

Materials ⏱ none

Divide the class into two groups, and assign each group a coin value, such as *nickel* or *dime*. Explain to students that you are going to tell them a certain amount of money. They then have to figure out how many nickels and dimes it would take to make that amount of money. For example, say *40 cents*. Ask the nickel group how many nickels make 40 cents. Then, ask the dime group how many dimes make 40 cents. Finally, ask the class how many nickels and dimes together make exactly 40 cents.

> **Teacher Tip**
>
> After a few rounds, have the groups trade their coin values. This way, all students get practice working with fives and tens. Invite less advanced students to use paper and pencil to help them. With more advanced students, designate groups as *quarter* and *half dollar*, and increase the total amounts of money.

Whose Number Is It?

Materials ⏱ none

Before beginning the game, write four numbers on the chalkboard. Invite four students to each stand under a number. Secretly select one of the numbers, and give clues to the rest of the class to see if they can figure out which student's number you are thinking of. For example, you might say *Whose number is a two-digit odd number?* or *Whose number is the same as 4 + 5?*

15   6   9   2

> **Teacher Tip**
>
> Instead of having the students stand under the number they selected, have them make up a clue to their number's identity. When the other students guess that number, then ask the student to go stand under it. For extra challenge and more simultaneous participation, play the game using more than four numbers and students.

Adjective Add-On

Materials ⏱ none

Use this activity to help students practice descriptive language. Choose an item or an object. As an example, say the name of the item and four describing words that tell how it looks (e.g., jack-o-lantern—orange, ugly, scary, spooky). Group students by tables, desks, rows, or in any other way they are seated. Assign each student group the name of an item, and ask each student to think of a word that describes that item. Before lining up or leaving, each group must share with the class a sentence that includes the name of the item and all the describing words.

Teacher Tip

As an alternative, ask each group to write down as many describing words as possible for their item. Dismiss first the group that compiles the longest list. For extra fun, choose classroom objects or items of students' clothing to describe.

Alphabet Logic

Materials ⏱ alphabet chart

Secretly choose a letter of the alphabet. Decide on positional clues to help students identify the letter, such as *The letter comes after d and before g and it is not f.* Invite the student or group that identifies the letter first to line up or move to the next activity.

Aa Bb Cc Dd Ee Ff Gg Hh Ii Jj

E!

Teacher Tip

Give students an opportunity to write clues during free time or at an independent learning center. This increases students' involvement and decreases your workload. Save students' suggestions for future use.

Animal Matchup

Materials ⏱ none

This activity requires students to visualize the spelling of simple phonetic words. Use the names of animals to dismiss students or have them move to the next activity. For example, you might say *If your name has one of the letters (sounds) in the word* cat, *you may line up.*

Teacher Tip

For less advanced students, make the clue more specific. For example, *If your name begins like* cat, *you may line up* or *If your name begins with any of the letters in* cat, *you may line up.*

Association Time

Materials ⏱ none

Have each student choose a color. Say the names of objects with an identifiable color, such as a banana, a cloud, or a stop sign. When an item matches the color a student selected, invite him or her to line up or move to the next activity.

Teacher Tip

Select a student to name the objects. For more advanced students, the name of the item could be spelled instead of stated aloud. Add variety by using other criteria, such as animals with feathers, fur, or scales; land, air, or sea animals; or countries in North America, Africa, or Asia.

Bingo Reading

Materials ⏱ none

Draw a five-by-five grid on the chalk-board or overhead projector. Write *BINGO* across the top, and number the boxes down the left side. Write a theme-related vocabulary word or a difficult high-frequency word in each box. Call out a letter and a number, and invite several student volunteers to read the word that falls in that box. Invite each student who reads a word correctly to line up or move to the next activity.

	B	**I**	**N**	**G**	**O**
1	orca	spout	calf	mammal	blubber
2	humpback	warm-blooded	breach	pod	whale
3	bull	krill	migration	barnacles	endangered
4	marine	cetacean	plankton	cow	blowhole
5	fluke	toothed	whaling	beluga	baleen

Teacher Tip

Once the students have the idea, allow them to take turns calling out letters and numbers. Reinforce spelling by having students write the word after reading it.

Build a Silly Sentence

Materials ⏱ none

Invite students to choose three words from a word list, and write them on the chalkboard. Ask the class to read the words, and then invite volunteers to make up sentences that include the three words. Write each sentence on the board, having students dictate the spelling. After awhile, only use adjectives to encourage the use of descriptive language. Invite volunteers who make up sentences to line up or move to the next activity.

Teacher Tip

When working with three adjectives, challenge students to create sentences in which the describing words are not next to each other. This will force them to include descriptive modifiers for three different nouns.

frog   hole   spoon

Expand It

Materials 🕐 none

Think of a compound word, but only say one part of the word (e.g., *bed* for *bedroom*). Invite the first student or group that comes up with an appropriate compound word to line up or move to the next activity.

Teacher Tip

Choose a volunteer to give the compound word clue. Have that student whisper the compound word and clue to you before saying it aloud. This will ensure that a workable clue is given.

man

manhole   fireman

Flashlight Favorites

Materials 🕐 direct-beam flashlight, alphabet chart

Shine a flashlight on one of the letters on an alphabet chart. Invite students whose name begins with that letter or sound to line up or move to the next activity.

Teacher Tip

Instead of beginning letters, have students line up when the last letter or sound of their name matches the one that is spotlighted.

l Mm Nn Oo Pp Qq Rr S

Phillip   Polly

It's All in a Name

Materials ⏱ none

Grant students permission to line up or move to the next activity by giving clues pertaining to the structure of or sounds in their names. For example:

Line up if your name has an odd number of letters in it.
Line up if your name is made up of ___ sounds. ___
Line up if your name has a short ___ in it.
Line up if your name has ___ syllable(s) in it.

Teacher Tip

Increase the difficulty of the clues by focusing on blends, digraphs, silent letters, or vowel combinations. You may also wish to use other clue patterns, such as last letters of names, hair or eye color, or gender.

Mystery Group

Materials ⏱ none

Tell students that you are going to select one of the class's cooperative groups to be the "mystery group." Secretly choose a group, and say the first letter of the name of each student in that group. Invite the first group to guess the identity of the mystery group to line up or move to the next activity.

Teacher Tip

Once students have figured out the clue pattern, invite volunteers to select the mystery group and give the clues.

Mary Nelson Oscar Patty

Name Patterns

Materials ⏱ none

Introduce this activity by saying that you will be using a special code to dismiss students. Write the following letters and symbol on the chalkboard: *B/G, V,* and *#.* Explain that the *B* stands for *boy,* the *G* for *girl, V* for a vowel sound, and the *#* stands for the number of syllables. Write an example, such as *B, /i/, 2,* and have students whose name follows this pattern stand up (e.g., Jimmy or William). Practice a few more times until students can quickly solve the code. Then, have students line up when their name matches the code.

One Step, No Prep © 1999 Creative Teaching Press

Teacher Tip

As an alternative, have students figure out their own code. Then, call on individuals to say their code and see if anyone else in the room has the same code.

Oh, That Alphabet!

Materials ⏱ none

Challenge students to name a letter and think of a three-word sentence in which two of the words begin with that letter and sound (e.g., *Billy is big* or *Susie is swimming*). Invite students to line up or move to the next activity after they recite a sentence. Once students master this, ask them to think of a three-word sentence in which all three words start with the chosen letter (e.g., *Jack just jumped* or *Donkeys dig dirt*). You may wish to first brainstorm words that begin with the letter as a class. Remind students that they can use the names of their classmates in their sentences.

One Step, No Prep © 1999 Creative Teaching Press

Teacher Tip

Give advanced students more specific directions. For example, require that the sentence include a name, one or more describing words, and an action word that all start with the chosen letter (e.g., *Pretty Patty plays piano, Cool Carlos collects coins,* or *Dingy Dan drives dangerously*). This is a good lesson to do in cooperative groups.

Opposites Roster

Materials ⏱ none

Divide the class into groups, and have students brainstorm common opposites. Write one of the words from several opposite pairs on the chalkboard. Have each student group select one of the words. Randomly choose one of the words from the list, and say its opposite. Invite the group that selected the appropriate opposite to line up or move to the next activity.

Teacher Tip

To reinforce word meaning and vocabulary development, substitute synonyms for opposites. When choosing vocabulary, use new words from shared-reading and guided-reading stories.

night
loud
even
small

odd

Pick and Choose

Materials ⏱ none

Choose three student volunteers to come to the front of the room. Have one of them name a consonant that can begin a three-letter word. Have the next student name a consonant that can end a three-letter word. Ask the last student to name a vowel sound that falls between the two consonants to create a real word. Invite a volunteer from the rest of the class to say the correct word and choose two new students to select two more consonant sounds. Then, have the first three students line up or move to the next activity. Invite the student who said the first complete word to name the vowel sound for the second word.

Teacher Tip

This activity is done orally to build phonemic awareness and blending skills. Try the activity with a visual "booster" by writing the consonants on the chalkboard. The vowel sound can still be said aloud.

b

g

short
i

Rhyming Chain

Materials ⏱ none

Divide the class into groups, or use pre-existing cooperative groups. Have a student from each group choose a word for the rhyming chain. Challenge each student from that group to come up with a word that rhymes with the group's first word. After students say their words aloud, invite them to line up and lock arms with the people in front of and behind them to form a whole-class rhyming chain.

Teacher Tip

For more advanced students, try the activity using synonyms, words with the same number of letters, or words with the same number of syllables instead of rhyming words.

One Step, No Prep © 1999 Creative Teaching Press

Roundup

Materials ⏱ none

Explain to students that, in this game, only certain items can be part of the "roundup." Secretly choose a specific letter pattern, such as the beginning sound /s/. Mention two things that can be rounded up (because they fit your secret pattern), and then say two things that cannot. For example, you might say *Sneakers and spaghetti can be rounded up, but balls and hats cannot.* Invite students who think they know the pattern to suggest something they think can be rounded up. Invite students who respond correctly to line up or move to the next activity.

Teacher Tip

Use more complicated sound patterns, such as ending sounds, medial vowel sounds, or polysyllabic words, for more advanced students.

One Step, No Prep © 1999 Creative Teaching Press

Secret Student

Materials ⏱ none

Give clues describing a student's name. For example, you might say *I'm thinking of a person whose name has one syllable, four letters, and the /oi/ sound.* When the secret student is identified, invite that student and the person who made the correct guess to line up or move to the next activity.

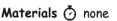

One Step, No Prep © 1999 Creative Teaching Press

Teacher Tip

Have more advanced students use a class list and make up identity clues. Write these clues on index cards, and place them in a grab bag for future use. For variety, use animal names instead of students' names.

Sing a Song of Sounds

Materials ⏱ none

Sing the following song to the tune of "If You're Happy and You Know It" when preparing students to leave the room:

If your name begins with ____, line up now.
If your name begins with ____, line up now.
If your name begins with ____, if your name begins with ____,
If your name begins with ____, line up now.

One Step, No Prep © 1999 Creative Teaching Press

Teacher Tip

For variety, use ending sounds, vowel sounds, or number of syllables. You may also wish to call out the sound of the letter rather than the letter name.

Syllable Count

Materials ⏱ word list, blank spinner (page 55)

In advance, create a 1–4 spinner. Assign a word from a word list to each student or cooperative group. Have a student volunteer spin the spinner. If a student or group's word contains that many syllables, invite them to line up or move to the next activity.

Teacher Tip

For early readers, use monosyllabic high-frequency words. Play the game counting phonemes rather than syllables.

Word Exchange

Materials ⏱ none

Begin this activity by defining the word *exchange*—to trade one thing for another. Explain to students that in this game you ask them to exchange letters within a word. Use examples such as the following:

⏱ Change the /o/ in *flop* to /i/. (flip)

⏱ Change the /t/ in *toy* to /b/. (boy)

⏱ Change the *in* in *fin* to *an*. (fan)

⏱ Say *string* without the *st*. (ring)

Invite the student or group that says the new word to line up or move to the next activity.

Teacher Tip

Make plans with an upper-grade teacher to have his or her class make up words for the "word exchange." This provides a useful phonemic-awareness lesson for the older students, too.

Climb the Ladder

Materials ⏱ none

Draw a five-rung ladder on the chalkboard for each student group. Write a different number on the top rung of each ladder. Ask each group to think of two numbers that, when added together, equal the number on their ladder. Encourage group members to brainstorm solutions together. When a group has found two numbers, write those numbers on the bottom and middle rungs. Write a plus sign and an equals sign on the second and fourth rungs, respectively. After a group "climbs" a ladder correctly, invite that group to line up or move to the next activity. Continue until all groups have identified two addends to go on a ladder.

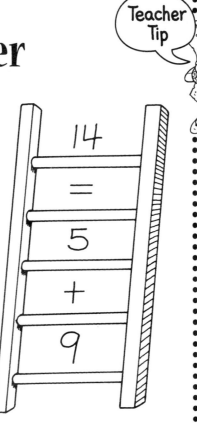

Teacher Tip

Once students are comfortable with this activity, use two numbers to make a missing-addend problem. Write the first addend on the first rung and the answer on the top rung. Challenge students to identify the second addend.

One Step, No Prep © 1999 Creative Teaching Press

Color-Coded Math

Materials ⏱ none

Draw a two-by-three grid on the chalkboard or overhead projector. Number the grid from 1 to 6 using a different color for each box. Have students take turns making addition problems by naming colors instead of numbers (e.g., *red + green*). Challenge the rest of the class to orally answer the problem. Invite students who create the addition problems to line up or move to the next activity.

Teacher Tip

This activity also makes an excellent inter-active bulletin board or learning center activity. Create a grid out of six sheets of different-colored construction paper, and write a different number on each sheet. Have students answer problems you create, or have them create, answer, and record their own color-coded addition problems.

One Step, No Prep © 1999 Creative Teaching Press

Double Digits

Materials ⏱ none

Write a plus sign and line on the chalkboard (to set up a vertical addition problem). Invite a student to write a two-digit number as the top number in the problem. Have another student write a second two-digit number directly under the first one. Ask a volunteer to write the answer to the problem. Then, have all three students line up or move to the next activity.

Teacher Tip

To give all students time to complete the problem, do not let students volunteer to write the answer until you raise your hand. Allow a few seconds of "think time" before raising your hand. Invite students to use pencil and paper to calculate answers, if necessary.

Find Your Partner

Materials ⏱ index cards

Prepare pairs of math-fact cards in which one card contains a problem and the other the solution. Randomly give each student a card, and, on your signal, have students mingle to find the person with the solution or problem that matches their card. When students find their partners, have them bring their cards to you and line up or move to the next activity.

Teacher Tip

Help students discover that many problems have the same answer and that there are many different ways to make a number. Try playing the game using only two or three numbers as possible solutions and many different problems that share those solutions. After students find a partner, have them find a new partner who also corresponds to their card.

High Man Low

Materials ⏱ none

Have each student select a number between 1 and 50 and write it on a scrap of paper. Tell students that they must listen to your cue to decide if they can line up or not. Use this format to provide the cues: *Line up if your number is higher than ___ but lower than ___.* Ask students to hand you their scraps of paper as they line up.

> **Teacher Tip**
>
> As the number of students remaining decreases, broaden the cues by saying, *Line up if your number is in the twenties/thirties/forties.* This reduces the time it takes to include all students in the game.

Is That You?

Materials ⏱ none

Assign each student a number for the week. Call students to line up based on their number, using methods such as the following:

⏱ Ask them to line up in sequence forwards or backwards.

⏱ Call up students whose number falls within a given range.

⏱ Count by twos to call the students up.

⏱ Say equations, and have the students line up when their number answers an equation.

> **Teacher Tip**
>
> This transition activity may take longer than others. Allow enough time so that all students are included and they do not lose time from their next activity.

MATH

Mystery Snakes

Materials ⏱ none

Draw on the chalkboard three or four snake-like configurations wide enough to write numbers inside. Add a dot for an eye on the left end. Draw lines to divide the snakes into segments. Add numbers inside each segment to create a pattern (a different pattern in each snake), but leave the last segment empty. Divide the class into groups, and assign each group a snake. Ask each group to figure out what number belongs in the last section of their snake. Once a group thinks they have discovered what the number should be, have one of the members write the number in the empty section. Ask the remaining groups to see if it is the correct number. Ask the group to explain why they chose that number. If their answer is correct, invite them to line up or move to the next activity.

MATH

Name That Number

Materials ⏱ none

Begin by saying a number aloud. Then, give a series of instructions that requires students to mentally alter that number by adding or subtracting. After giving several instructions, challenge students to "name that number." For example, say *Start with three. Now add four. Now take away two. Name that number!* Select that number of students to line up or move to the next activity.

Number Houses

Materials ⏱ none

Draw on the chalkboard a house large enough to write in. Write a number inside the roof section. Ask each group to think of an equation whose answer is the same number as the one in the house. As each group gives an equation, write the equation in the house, and have that group line up. Depending on the level of the class, encourage students to give problems that include all four operations.

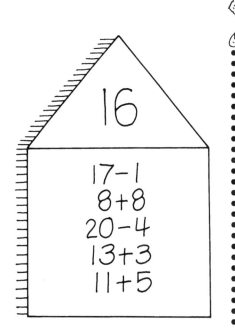

16

17 − 1
8 + 8
20 − 4
13 + 3
11 + 5

Teacher Tip

After students are familiar with this activity, give each group a piece of paper. Draw a house on the board, and ask the groups to copy it. Then, write a number in the roof section. Have the groups "race" to see who can finish listing all possible answers first.

Read My Mind

Materials ⏱ none

Give oral clues that require students to mentally compute the number you are thinking of. For example, you might say *I'm thinking of a number that is more than six but less than ten. If you add two to that number, you get nine. Read my mind. What number am I thinking of?* Invite that number of students to line up or move to the next activity.

Read my mind. What number am I thinking of?

Teacher Tip

Give students adequate thinking time to calculate the solution. Remind them to think silently and only respond when you ask for the answer. This gives all students an opportunity to participate without feeling intimidated by faster students. Increase the level of difficulty depending on the ability level of your students.

The Same As

Materials ⏱ none

Divide the class into groups, and have them count by tens to 100. Assign each group a tens number. Call groups to line up or move to the next activity by saying *You may line up if your number is the same as ___ tens.* Continue in this manner, calling each table or group's number.

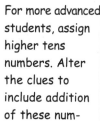

For more advanced students, assign higher tens numbers. Alter the clues to include addition of these numbers, such as three tens plus five tens.

Say It First

Materials ⏱ none

Write a three-addend equation frame on the chalkboard. Choose three students to write a number between 0 and 6 on a blank in the equation. Have students raise their hand when they have solved the problem. Invite the first person who gives the correct answer to line up or move to the next activity.

Instead of having students choose a number, ask them a simple addition problem, and have them write the answer in the equation frame (e.g., say *2 + 1*, so students write *3* in the equation). After all three addends have been written in the equation frame, have students solve the three-addend addition problem. In addition, you may wish to have more advanced students work with multiple operations (e.g., 7 – 4 + 3).

Story-Problem Chain

Materials ⏱ none

Begin the process by saying a story problem that involves students' names. For example, you might say *I have four cookies, but I gave two to Jenna.* Invite that student to create a new story problem based on that same information, such as *I had two cookies and I got two more, so now I have four cookies. But I'm giving one cookie to Ethan.* Invite each student mentioned to continue the story-problem chain.

Teacher Tip

Use this activity to transition children from one activity to another by dismissing each student after he or she recites a story problem.

Sum's Up

Materials ⏱ none

Have each student or group write on scratch paper a number between 0 and 9. Tell students that when their number answers an equation you give, they may stand up, say the answer, and line up or move to the next activity. Say simple addition equations aloud, such as $2 + 3 = \_\_\_$.

Teacher Tip

Have different students select and say the problem. Invite more advanced students to choose higher numbers, such as numbers between 10 and 20 or any number in the forties.

Spinners

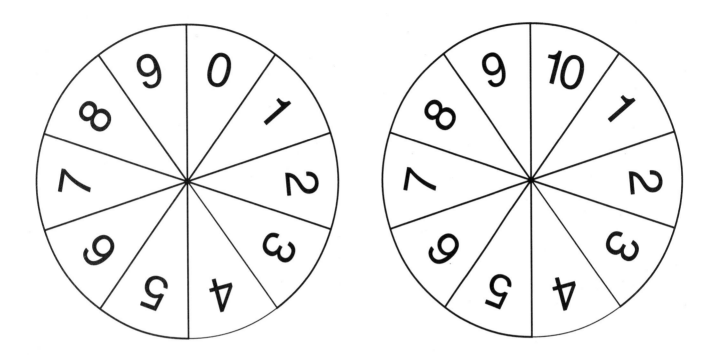

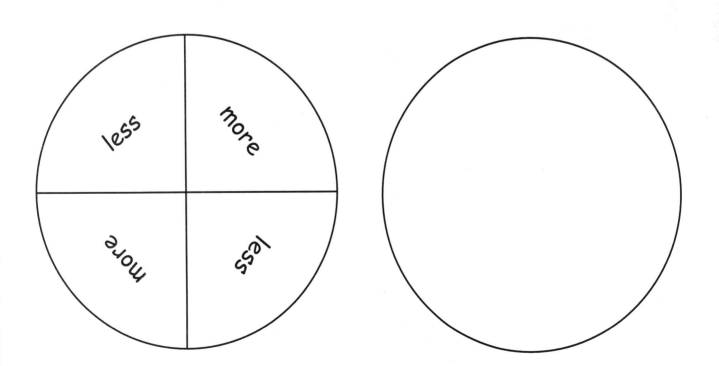

Word Families

-ab: cab, dab, jab, tab, blab, crab, grab, scab

-ack: back, pack, rack, sack, tack, black, crack, quack, shack, snack, stack, track

-ad: bad, dad, had, lad, mad, pad, sad, glad

-ade: fade, made, blade, grade, shade, spade, trade

-ag: bag, nag, rag, sag, tag, wag, brag, drag, flag, shag, snag

-ail: bail, fail, hail, mail, nail, pail, rail, sail, tail, wail, frail, snail, trail

-ain: gain, main, pain, rain, brain, chain, drain, grain, plain, stain, train

-air: air, fair, hair, pair, chair, stair

-ake: bake, cake, fake, lake, make, rake, take, wake, brake, quake, shake, snake, stake

-am: am, ham, jam, ram, yam, clam, cram, gram, slam, swam, wham

-ame: came, fame, game, lame, name, same, tame, blame, flame, frame, shame

-an: an, can, fan, man, pan, ran, tan, van, plan, scan, than

-and: and, band, hand, land, sand, grand, stand

-ang: bang, fang, hang, rang, sang, clang

-ank: bank, sank, tank, blank, crank, drank, thank

-ap: cap, gap, lap, map, nap, rap, sap, tap, clap, flap, slap, snap, trap, wrap, strap

-ape: ape, cape, tape, grape, shape, scrape

-ar: bar, car, far, jar, tar, scar, star

-ark: ark, bark, dark, lark, mark, park, shark, spark

-art: art, cart, dart, part, tart, chart, smart, start

One Step, No Prep © 1999 Creative Teaching Press

Word Families

-ash: ash, cash, dash, lash, mash, rash, crash, flash, slash, smash, trash, splash

-at: at, bat, cat, fat, hat, mat, pat, rat, sat, vat, chat, flat, that

-ate: ate, date, fate, gate, hate, late, mate, crate, plate, skate, state

-ay: bay, day, hay, lay, may, pay, ray, say, way, clay, gray, play, pray, stay, sway, spray, stray

-eal: deal, heal, meal, real, seal, steal, squeal

-eam: beam, seam, team, cream, dream, steam, scream, stream

-eat: eat, beat, heat, meat, neat, seat, treat, wheat

-ed: bed, fed, led, red, wed, fled, shed, sled, shred

-ee: bee, fee, see, free, knee, tree, three

-eed: feed, need, seed, weed, bleed, speed

-eel: eel, feel, heel, peel, kneel, steel, wheel

-eep: beep, deep, jeep, keep, peep, weep, creep, sheep, sleep, steep, sweep

-eet: beet, feet, meet, greet, sheet, sleet, sweet, street

-ell: bell, cell, fell, sell, tell, well, yell, shell, smell, spell, swell

-en: den, hen, men, pen, ten, then, when

-ent: bent, cent, dent, rent, sent, tent, vent, went, scent, spent

-ess: less, mess, bless, chess, dress, guess, press

-est: best, jest, nest, pest, rest, test, vest, west, chest, guest, quest

-et: bet, get, jet, let, met, net, pet, set, vet, wet, yet, fret

-ew: dew, few, new, blew, chew, crew, drew, flew, grew, knew, stew, screw, threw

Word Families

-ice: ice, dice, lice, mice, nice, rice, price, slice, spice, twice

-ick: kick, lick, pick, sick, tick, brick, chick, click, flick, quick, slick, stick, thick, trick

-id: bid, did, hid, kid, lid, rid, grid, skid, slid, squid

-ide: hide, ride, side, tide, wide, bride, glide, pride, slide

-ig: big, dig, fig, jig, pig, rig, wig, twig

-ight: fight, light, might, night, right, sight, bright, flight

-ill: ill, bill, fill, gill, hill, mill, pill, will, chill, drill, grill, skill, spill, still, thrill

-im: dim, him, rim, grim, slim, trim

-ime: dime, lime, mime, time, chime, crime, grime, prime, slime

-in: in, bin, fin, kin, pin, tin, win, chin, grin, shin, skin, spin, thin, twin

-ing: king, ring, sing, wing, bring, cling, sling, sting, swing, thing, spring, string

-ink: link, mink, pink, rink, sink, wink, blink, drink, stink, think, shrink

-ip: dip, hip, lip, rip, sip, tip, chip, clip, drip, flip, grip, ship, skip, slip, snip, trip, whip

-it: it, bit, fit, hit, kit, lit, pit, sit, grit, knit, quit, skit, slit, spit, split

-ive: dive, five, hive, live, drive

-oat: boat, coat, goat, bloat, float, throat

-ock: dock, lock, rock, sock, block, clock, flock, knock, shock, smock, stock

-og: dog, fog, hog, jog, log, clog, frog, smog

-oil: oil, boil, coil, foil, soil, broil, spoil

-oke: joke, poke, woke, broke, choke, smoke, spoke, stroke

One Step, No Prep © 1999 Creative Teaching Press

Word Families

-old: old, bold, cold, gold, hold, mold, sold, told, scold

-ole: hole, mole, pole, role, stole, whole

-one: bone, cone, lone, tone, zone, phone, stone

-ool: cool, fool, pool, tool, spool, stool, school

-oom: boom, room, zoom, bloom, broom, groom

-oon: loon, moon, noon, soon, spoon

-op: hop, mop, pop, top, chop, crop, drop, flop, shop, stop

-ose: hose, nose, rose, close, those

-ot: cot, dot, got, hot, lot, not, pot, rot, tot, knot, plot, spot, trot

-ub: cub, hub, rub, sub, tub, club, grub, stub, scrub, shrub

-uck: buck, duck, luck, puck, tuck, cluck, pluck, stuck, truck, struck

-uff: cuff, huff, muff, puff, bluff, fluff, stuff

-ug: bug, dug, hug, jug, mug, rug, tug, drug, plug, slug, snug, shrug

-um: bum, gum, hum, mum, sum, yum, drum, plum, strum

-ump: bump, dump, hump, jump, lump, pump, plump, stump, thump

-un: bun, fun, pun, run, sun, spun

-unch: bunch, hunch, lunch, munch, punch, crunch

-ush: hush, mush, rush, blush, brush, flush, slush

-ust: bust, dust, gust, just, must, rust, crust, trust

-ut: but, cut, hut, nut, shut, strut

-y: by, my, cry, fly, fry, ply, sly, try, why

Puzzle Grid

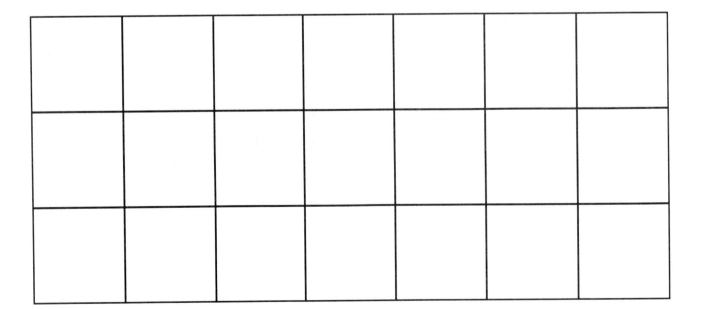

Number Cards (1-4)

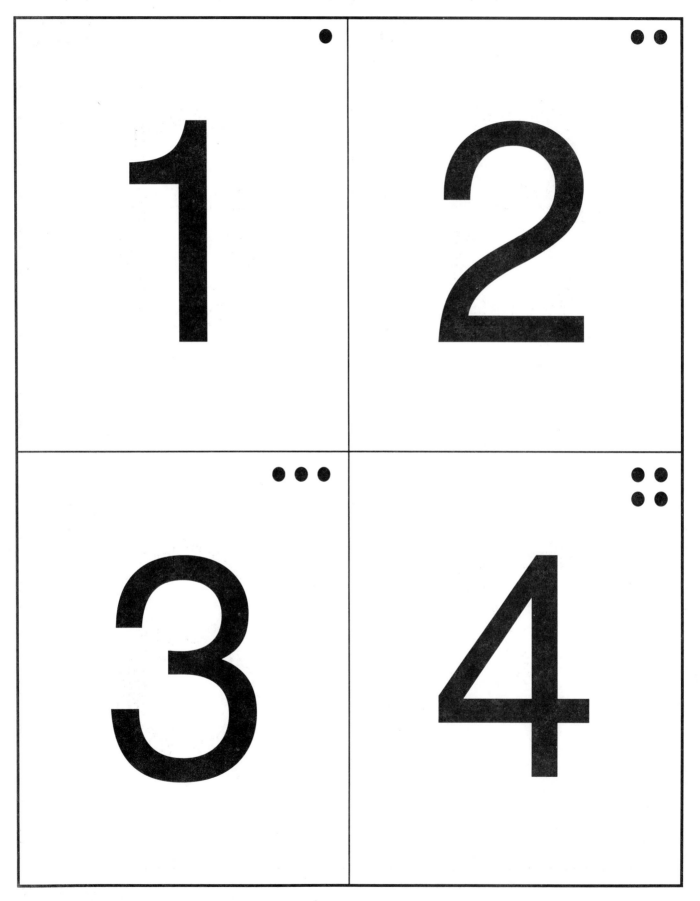

One Step, No Prep © 1999 Creative Teaching Press

Number Cards (5-8)

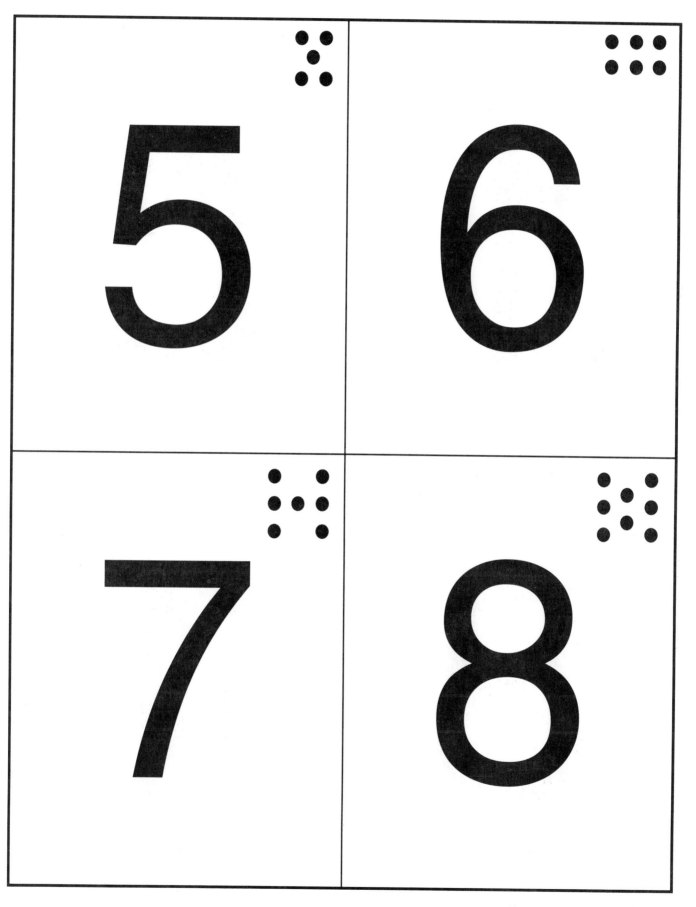

Number Cards (9-12)

One Step, No Prep © 1999 Creative Teaching Press